D1112425

AMICA'S WORLD

HOW A GIANT BIRD CAME INTO OUR HEART AND HOME

WASHO AND **MEADOW SHADOWHAWK**
FOREWORD BY **DR. JANE GOODALL**

MICROCOSM PUBLISHING
PORTLAND, OR

AMICA'S WORLD
HOW A GIANT BIRD CAME INTO OUR HEART AND HOME

photos and text © Washo and Meadow Shadowhawk, 2014-2016
This edition © Microcosm Publishing, 2016

For a catalog, write or visit:
Microcosm Publishing
2752 N Williams Ave.
Portland, OR 97227
MicrocosmPublishing.com

ISBN 978-1-62106-282-0
First Published November 15, 2016
First printing of 5,000 copies
This is Microcosm #259

Distributed by Legato / Perseus Books Group and Turnaround, U.K.
Printed on post-consumer paper

Global labor conditions are bad, and our roots in industrial Cleveland in the 70s and 80s made us appreciate the need to treat workers right. Therefore, our books are MADE IN THE USA

Library of Congress Cataloging-in-Publication Data
Names: Shadowhawk, Washo, author. | Shadowhawk, Meadow, author.
Title: Amica's world : how a giant bird came into our heart and home / Washo and Meadow Shadowhawk ; foreword by Dr. Jane Goodall.
Description: Portland, OR : Microcosm Publishing, 2016.
Identifiers: LCCN 2016003106 (print) | LCCN 2016034747 (ebook) | ISBN 9781621062820 (pbk.) | ISBN 9781621069164 (epdf) | ISBN 9781621068440 (epub) | ISBN 9781621069317 (kindle)
Subjects: LCSH: Greater rhea--Oregon--Beaverton. | Human-animal relationships.
Classification: LCC QL696.R4 S53 20169 (print) | LCC QL696.R4 (ebook) | DDC 636.6--dc23
LC record available at https://lccn.loc.gov/2016003106

AMICA'S WORLD

HOW A GIANT BIRD CAME INTO OUR HEART AND HOME

WASHO AND MEADOW SHADOWHAWK
FOREWORD BY DR. JANE GOODALL

FOREWORD
DR. JANE GOODALL

As you read this book and study the photographs you will gradually fall in love. For Amica is truly loveable. More than that, he is extremely intelligent and a great source of entertainment.

I have known the Shadowhawk family for many years, and I have long known about Washo's love of all animals—I believe that, just as I was, he was born with that love. And, again like myself, he had an understanding and supportive mother, Meadow. It was she, along with Washo's father, who showed me photographs of the infant Washo with various pets. The one I remember most is a duckling—they had a very close bond.

As he grew older, Washo sometimes rescued exotic animals that would otherwise, almost certainly, have died because they were being treated in highly inappropriate ways by owners of pet shops. He told me how he talked to people who were thinking of buying some exotic—and utterly inappropriate—animal, explaining the problems they would encounter. He rescued many snakes that had been wounded—often by dogs—and released them once they were well again. Except one female, who could never be returned to the wild, but who helped him cure new arrivals—but that is another remarkable story, that I hope he will write.

From the start, I was impressed by the connection Washo made with his animal companions. He forged such close bonds with a bearded dragon that she demonstrated by very different behaviors that she actually shared his moods. Compared with reptiles, birds are in a whole different category. Perhaps Washo was in some way prepared for his relationship with Amica as a result of the very close bond he developed as a small child with his duck.

I never really thought much about rheas before, and I have been enchanted over several years to receive updates about Amica's behavior. What an utterly charming individual. I am really glad that Washo decided to write this book. And you, the reader, will be glad also—you are in for a treat.

INTRODUCTION

This is the story of how our family raised Amica in our home. The name Amica is pronounced ah-MEEK-uh and is the Latin word for "friend." Amica is a rhea—a large, flightless bird.

Living with Amica changed our life. But we do not recommend raising a rhea in your own home. As you will see, it requires many sacrifices and accommodations, and can be dangerous to both you and the animal if precautions are not taken. We are sharing our story because we want to show you what we have learned about this amazing bird.

One of the challenges we experienced was photographing Amica. We had a quality DSLR camera that took high resolution photos in low light, but had to take many photos with our phones, as the large camera proved too distracting for Amica to behave in his usual manner. He is very curious and aware of anything. If he finds anything unusual he may spend hours investigating it. We have lost many great photo opportunities to this curiosity.

WHAT ARE RHEAS?

Rheas are part of a diverse group of flightless birds known as ratites. While the ostrich and emu are perhaps the most widely known ratites, the group ranges from the chicken-sized kiwi to the now-extinct, twelve-foot tall, five-hundred-pound giant moa.

Although species of ratites can be found on several continents throughout the world, not much is known about them. If you were to ask most people for a fact about an ostrich or emu, they would most likely tell you something like, "they bury their heads in the sand when they become frightened" which is not true. After spending a little over a year with a live ratite, it seems the few "facts" that we humans thought we knew may not be accurate.

So why do we know so little about these animals? Perhaps one reason is that due to the shy nature of ratites, it can be difficult for researchers in the field to get close enough to the birds to study their behavior. Another issue could be that since most ratites have developed very specific adaptations to allow them to survive in their natural habitats, they cannot thrive outside of the environment they were designed for. For example, the ostrich, designed for the open and arid land of the African savannas, does not do well in damper climates where their two-toed feet cannot support their heavy bodies in the mud. In contrast, the cassowary, which is native to the humid rainforests of New Guinea, could not survive in drier climates without access to their primary diet of fungi and fruit.

One exception to this fragility among ratites is the rhea. Native to South America and ranging from Brazil to Argentina, the rhea has been able to adapt to a wide range of environments. In relation to other ratites, the rhea's median size and weight seem to have made it by far the most adaptable species. According to current records, wild rheas stand about five feet tall and can weigh up to 90 pounds (although ours has surpassed those numbers in both height and weight). They have three toes on each foot, which provides better traction and support, as well as plumage that covers most of their body, providing insulation and allowing them to thrive in colder climates than other ratites.

A THREATENED SPECIES

A common cause of death for all ratites is being hunted or harvested for food by humans. Ostrich and emu meat, especially as jerky, is a popular exotic meat, and unfortunately, since rheas are smaller and hardier, they have proven to be an even more attractive source of ratite meat.

Wild rheas that live in their native habitat have a very high mortality rate in their first year. In the first three months of their life, rhea chicks are extremely delicate—especially their legs, which are still developing. A main tendon in the leg has to set in place within the knee joint. If the bird falls or trips in these first few months, the tendon can pop out of place and the legs can become permanently damaged. Since ratites are flightless birds, they rely on their legs as other birds rely on their wings. Rhea chicks have been observed to walk over a mile a day, and it is by walking and running that the chicks develop their bodies properly. In the wild, when a chick injures a leg it cannot run with the others or forage for food. Unable to move, if they manage to not be eaten by a predator, they slowly starve to death.

Rheas that survive to adulthood face another danger. The gaucho people of South America have a long-standing tradition of hunting rheas for both food and sport. As a result, rheas are now rated as a threatened species and only those living outside of their native land have been known to prosper. Most rheas are now seen as livestock animals and are raised in large flocks only to be slaughtered once they reach the desired size. However, every now and then a few rheas escape from the meat farms and have managed to thrive in the foreign wilderness. One such example took place in the late 1990s in northeastern Germany. A small number of rheas escaped from an exotic meat farm in Lubeck and have since adapted and reproduced into a flock of well over a hundred living throughout the eastern countryside.

Although not as common or profitable as the meat farms, there are a few less depressing examples of humans' relationship with rheas. Recently, a few ranches in Oregon and New Mexico have discovered that rheas can provide more commodities than just meat. Their eggs, which are much larger and thicker than that of a chicken, can be eaten, or the shells can be blown out and used for carving and other works of art. Rhea feathers are unique and come in a variety of different sizes and colors making them ideal for a multitude of uses (rheas shed their feathers constantly).

Perhaps the best examples of non-food-related rhea domestication have come from England. Prior to caring for our own rhea, the best sources of information were found from ranches throughout England that had taken a different approach to raising these birds. They were treated similarly to the way some of us treat chickens, more like pets and less like food. Most rheas had regular human interaction and were often handled and carried around not long after hatching. Some of the older birds were even used in the same manner as we use goats. The rheas were transported in horse trailers to overgrown farmland and were released in an enclosed area. With the birds' voracious appetite, the area was quickly cleared out enough that the farmers could finish the job with a lot less work. The rheas benefited, the farmers benefited, and the only things that were eaten were the weeds. These are just a few examples of the many ways humans could benefit from better understanding these animals.

After researching ratites and preparing to take on the task of caring for one, we knew it would be a unique journey. However, we had expected that our knowledge and experience of rehabilitating and caring for a variety of animals throughout the years would provide us with most of the tools necessary for the task. Together, our family has cared for not only wild and exotic birds, but horses, llamas, reptiles, various kinds of small mammals, as well as your more common dogs and cats. How different could one ratite be?

Apparently, very different.

This book is in no way intended as a how-to guide for raising a rhea. Ratites are completely unlike any cat, dog, horse, or other type of bird. Amica stands six feet tall and can open doors and drawers, so we have had to "rhea-proof" our house and yard to keep him as well as others safe.

When we first brought Amica home everyone believed he was a female (though it is very difficult to determine at this age) so we gave him a feminine name. After six months it became obvious that he was, in fact, a male. He was already accustomed to his name and he was still our "friend" so we did not change it.

Within the last year and a half that Amica has lived with us, he has shown more recognizable personality and intelligence than we have ever personally witnessed from an animal. But while Amica has enriched our lives in many ways, the rare experience of caring for such an animal doesn't come without compromise.

After getting through the nerve-racking three-month delicate phase of infancy, he transitioned into puberty. For a bird, this includes establishing pecking order within the flock by fighting for dominancy. At this point, being considered by a rhea to be part of the flock isn't such a good thing. For several months, Amica's behavior was very similar to that of the velociraptors from Jurassic Park—clearly not the ideal family pet. Eventually, that phase passed as well, leaving us with a few battle scars. Now, Amica spends most of his energy digging nests in the backyard as well as being much more demanding of our company.

While this animal takes a great deal of attention, patience, space, and money, he gives back by providing an insight into the complex behavior of these fascinating creatures that most people are not even familiar with, and if they are, they think of them as livestock.

PART ONE
A DELICATE
YOUNG BIRD

Amica is in one of three eggs that hatch on July 1, 2014 at the Richey Ranch in Lebanon, Oregon. If he had been hatched in his natural habitat, he would have been surrounded by about a dozen siblings and raised by his father on a rocky hillside in South America.

All three appear to be females, though sexing the birds at this age is not an exact science. Amica is the one with the white patch on the top of his head and deep blue eyes standing in the corner.

Amica is just over one week old when we bring him home. Most rheas do not live for more than three months so we take special precautions to provide him with a safe environment and diet.

At home, we introduce him to the pen area we have prepared. A soft mat is on the floor to prevent him from slipping. He has an open box to sleep in, and special food and water bowls. It is all surrounded by a three-foot-high fence to keep him safe and make him feel secure.

Exercise is important for proper development and Amica is constantly on the go.

We soon discover that it would be in his best interest to open his pen to include the entire living room, allowing him more room to exercise his long legs.

We originally planned to move Amica to a pen in the back yard with the chickens, who would become his flock. But after a few days in our living room, it becomes evident that we are the ones who have been accepted as his new flock when he approaches and eventually lays down on a pillow next to Washo.

A rhea chick in the wild would spend the first six months of its life with its father learning to find food, build nests, and just survive. Amica enjoys sleeping in his box at night once the lights go out but still protests being alone.

A baby gate keeps ever curious Amica contained in a safe area. Amica loves watching television with the family. We haven't figured out why, but he seems to prefer shows where the characters speak with an English accent. One of his favorites is Downton Abbey on Masterpiece. He stays up long past his bedtime to watch it.

Birds grow very rapidly. By his third month, Amica needs even more room to play during the day.

So we fence off a portion of the back yard for him to explore during the day. He is never alone in this outdoor space. We have to watch him carefully to make sure he doesn't break a leg or eat something harmful.

The warm summer sun is a new experience as Amica has spent most of his young life indoors

He raises his wings for many reasons: for relief from the heat, to look threatening, or in this case, just stretching out his feathers and relaxing.

The stripes on the back of Amica's body provide camouflage. We do not know for sure, but we doubt that birds in the wild would adopt this sleeping position.

We reposition the portable fence we built to expand Amica's outdoor enclosure, giving him more room to run.

The fence is now placed to keep Amica out of the soft ground in the garden, where he could easily break his delicate legs. I don't think he understands why the chickens are allowed to be on the other side.

The chickens are a great source of fun for Amica. The only problem is that he insists on trying to remove the red bits from around their faces, which is not appreciated by the chickens.

There is no shortage of companions to keep him company. Besides the humans and chickens, there are also two cats, a dog, assorted wild birds, and the occasional squirrel. He finds the squirrels most entertaining, as they play chasing games with him around the trunk of the apple tree.

The dog is great fun, since he can run almost as fast as Amica and is willing to at any opportunity.

Soon Amica is towering over his rooster companions, but this doesn't seem to affect the friendship.

Over his first two months, Amica's feathers start to change and he begins to lose the fluffy chick feathers but still maintains his deep blue eyes and the white flash on the top of his head.

Rheas are omnivores, which means they eat just about anything. Amica has a very special diet for the first three months to prevent the digestive problems that can prove fatal in rhea chicks. His breakfast is a small amount of beef heart mixed with pineapple, carrots and cabbage, and he always has a bowl of crumbled poultry food available throughout the day. He also eats grass and the occasional bug. He loves it when the apples begin to fall from the tree, and runs out every morning to find them. When he does he picks them up and throws them to the ground one by one to break them into smaller pieces so that he can eat them.

Amica is getting a little frizzy at this awkward age. His striped camouflage feathers are slowly being replaced by new, adult feathers.

It's fall and while helping us to rake the leaves in the back yard, Amica decides we are working on building a nest. We don't have the heart to rake up the nest of leaves he has gathered—he seems so proud of himself.

Blue eyes are common for the white rheas but not for the grey variety. We learned that a male rhea on Richey's Ranch also has blue eyes and a white marking on his head. His name is "Demon" and he is an alpha male among the flock and most likely Amica's father.

By December, Amica is nearly six months old and stands almost five feet tall. We can't have a Christmas tree in our living room because Amica would remove and most likely eat the ornaments and even the branches. So we are grateful when he ignores the garland hung over the window in an attempt to make things festive.

PART TWO
VELOCIRAPTOR

By summer, Amica is reaching maturity and we see a change in his behavior as he is trying to establish his place in the flock and begins challenging us for pecking order. The backyard becomes his territory and anyone entering is challenged. He charges with his wings up high over his back, beak open, and at a full run.

Many people believe rheas are descended from dinosaurs. When you are being chased by one, you can see the resemblance.

It is disturbing to witness that even the small birds, once a source of entertainment, are now hunted and eaten.

We are grateful that this new aggression does not extend to the chickens and that they are still friends.

Fortunately for all of us, the aggression stops at the door when Amica enters for the night and everyone is friendly again.

Every evening, Amica comes back in the house. As he enters, he stops at the area rug just inside the door and take a dust bath using the rug.

This rug bath can last for a long time, as he is quite thorough in his efforts to reach all of his feathers.

Sometimes the rug doesn't cooperate.

When the dust bath is complete, he begins to explore. Meadow's desk is a favorite place because he can find small objects to carry off in his beak, causing everyone to jump up and retrieve them.

Much like a canine companion, Amica enjoys lying next to someone just relaxing in the living room.

As the evening winds down, Amica goes to a corner of the living room and gets comfortable for the night.

Just before he goes to sleep each night, Amica preens all of his feathers into place. As his coloring changes, he starts to molt and beautiful feathers from one half inch to over one foot in length start coming out. In the morning when he goes outside, we gather a beautiful collection of feathers.

Rheas' ears open and shut as needed—Amica's ears are shut here as he settles down to sleep. And their eyelids close upward. When Amica's eyes are shut, his eyelashes are at the top of his eyes.

Amica is out for the night, but not unaware—his ears are open.

We are relieved that Amica's outdoor aggression only lasts as long as breeding season—about three months. By September, he has become inquisitive and friendly again—and very hungry for our affection.

PART THREE
OUR LOVING AND
CURIOUS FRIEND

Amica spends a lot of time at the sliding glass door, watching the daily routine going on inside.

Trying to convince the cat to come outside and play...through the glass door.

Separated by the fence, Amica still doesn't understand why the chickens are allowed to be over there.

Here Amica is helping Washo gather the sunflowers. Normally he is fenced off from this part of the yard to keep the small birds that eat the sunflowers safe. We were surprised to learn that Amica loves to eat sunflowers.

Amica decides to pick the sunflowers himself.

Under Washo's supervision, Amica explores previously-restricted areas.

After discovering how much Amica likes to eat sunflowers Washo starts feeding them to him to make sure that he doesn't eat any that are too big.

Amica with a lump in his throat. I always thought when the ostrich in the cartoons swallowed a ball and you could watch the ball shaped lump go down its long neck that it was just make believe. Well, it's not!

Amica and Wiyaka the family dog are good friends. They both feel a need to protect the family. Both will alert us when someone is approaching, but Amica can always hear them first.

Anyone living in the Pacific Northwest knows how important it is to enjoy the sun while you can.

Amica will sit in the grass and preen for hours, enjoying the warmth on his feathers.

Rheas are as graceful as a ballet dancer; well at least once they are fully grown. When they are young they trip over their long legs and crash into everything. Amica loves to run, dart from side to side and hop into the air with the speed of a cheetah. He stops just short of crashing into the fence ...well, at least most of the time.

He loves racing around the back yard in front of the chickens. They are not sure what to make of him when he does this.

It is easy to see why a running rhea would remind someone of the Road Runner in the Wile E. Coyote cartoon.

Feathers flying, Amica rounds the corner, just missing the apple tree.

Amica can turn on a dime.

After a good run in the yard, it's time to preen the feathers back into place.

His strong legs are built for running.

It is the father rhea that builds the nests, hatches the eggs, and raises the babies. Amica is a great nest builder. At first, he gathered the dead leaves from the bushes to line his nest, however now he pulls out the live ones as well and it has left huge holes in the landscaping that surrounds the yard.

Once he decides the nest is suitable, he will try it out. Even his friends are not welcome at this point.

After a hard day of nest building, a bird can get pretty muddy. We haven't figured out how to teach him to wipe his feet, so we try to keep him on his area rug long enough to get most of the mud off.

Amica has just entered the house after a cold and very rainy day, the feathers on his back so wet they are stuck together revealing bare skin. There is a heat lamp just outside the sliding door next to my desk where he lays and you can see the mud he shook off earlier in the day on the glass. His belly is still wet and muddy but he will preen that out when he takes his area rug bath, however, first he must greet Kota his feline friend. They often sleep together at night.

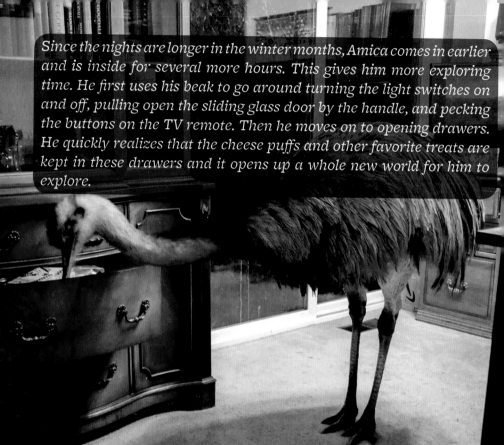

Since the nights are longer in the winter months, Amica comes in earlier and is inside for several more hours. This gives him more exploring time. He first uses his beak to go around turning the light switches on and off, pulling open the sliding glass door by the handle, and pecking the buttons on the TV remote. Then he moves on to opening drawers. He quickly realizes that the cheese puffs and other favorite treats are kept in these drawers and it opens up a whole new world for him to explore.

s a favorite place to explore as there are so many drawers and
ecks at the keyboard it makes the monitor change pictures.

Amica wants to be wherever the family is, but areas like the kitchen are just not safe. A slippery floor and too many dangerous things to go in his mouth make this room off limits. A thick piece of cardboard goes up to block the entry before he comes in each night. He does not approve.

Amica loves to be pet, and will even approach the dog and cats in an effort to have his neck rubbed. Now an adult, his wingspan is about six feet.

Amica is protesting that the television is not turned on; he might be missing his favorite show. He seems to enjoy murder mysteries, Masterpiece Theater, and occasionally college football. Sometimes if a food commercial comes on the screen he will get up and try to eat whatever is being shown and we have to race to change the channel before he succeeds.

...a strange vocalization that sounds like an elephant playing ...When they make this sound, they strike an upright posture ...est out and every feather vibrates as they produce a long, ...ued humming noise.

So many feathers, and they all require a good preening.

Especially in those hard-to-reach places.

Much like when a dog comes to your side and begs to be pet, Amica will approach someone sitting on the couch with his neck down and wings out—his way of asking for someone to rub his neck.

He's a flock animal, and we're his flock.

When you just can't reach that itchy spot on the side of your head.

Rhea feathers are prized by artists who use them in their crafts. Amica's feathers are beautifully trimmed in silver and come in many shapes and lengths.

Here he is getting comfortable after his show is over. Sometimes his head will slowly drop until his beak hits the pillow then falls to the side at which point he wakes up and tucks his head between his shoulder blades

Amica exhibits many emotions with his expressive face and body language. Sometimes he looks downright sarcastic.

This is the face you get when it's the weekend and his favorite show is not on.

His puffy cheeks and bushy eyebrows make him almost irresistible.

Here is his look of contentment as he lies in the grass in the sun.

Amica is so excited as the snow begins to fall that he acts like a young child as he runs around trying to catch the falling snowflakes in his beak.

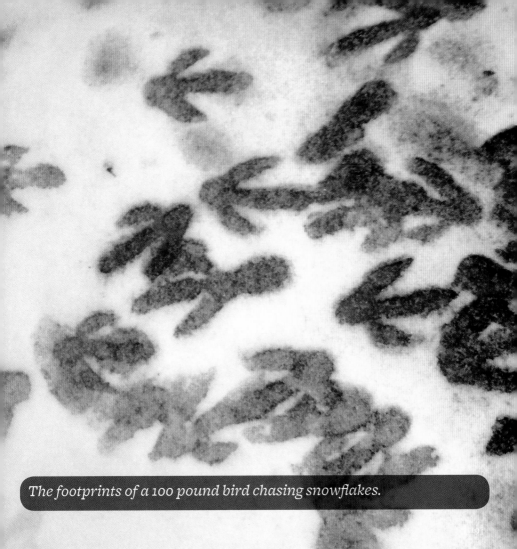

The footprints of a 100 pound bird chasing snowflakes.

We have watched Amica grown from a small chick into a graceful

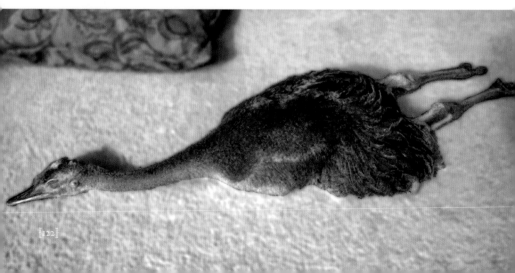

adult and he has become an integral part of our family in the process.

Our journey with Amica is just beginning and with his life expectancy of about 40 years, it will hopefully be a long and happy one.

AFTERWORD

Our family would never suggest raising a rhea in your home. Animals thrive best in their own natural habitat. Amica's upbringing was unique, and living with him continues to require major sacrifices on our part.

While working as a veterinarian technician, assisting as an intern at the zoo, and helping with rescued animals, our family has witnessed some incredible animals of every kind. A bearded dragon that helped care for baby mice, a garter snake that would drag other injured snakes to a food source, a full grown Hereford bull that thought he was a lap dog and even a cat that gave half of her four week old litter of kittens to her dog friend who was in mourning because her puppies were stillborn. Animals are capable of far more than we humans can imagine.

Amica's story is a reminder that all animals are amazing creatures: intelligent, loving, and compassionate beings deserving of respect. As humans, we need to be mindful of how we treat all living things in our care, as it affects not only us but the world we live in. Livestock animals, when humanely raised with sustainable methods, are not only happier themselves but provide healthier meat, eggs, and dairy products for humans. Even the land they are raised on is positively impacted. Perhaps Amica will become an ambassador of livestock animals all over the world, helping people recognize the need to change the way the majority of livestock animals are raised.

ABOUT THE AUTHORS

Washo Shadowhawk has been working with and helping animals from a very young age. When he was 14, Dr. Jane Goodall recognized his work doing outreach to zoo primates and nominated him for the IDA Youth Guardian Award, which he won. He was featured on the Animal Planet movie "Jane Goodall's Heroes" as one of her heroes and was the recipient of the Gloria Barron Prize for young heroes. He lives in Oregon, where he is a photographer and runs a rescue operation for exotic reptiles and birds.

Meadow Shadowhawk is Washo's mother. She has a background as a veterinarian technician and also enjoys working with animals. She shares Washo's love of nature and has always supported his love of animals.

Dr. Jane Goodall is the world's preeminent primatologist, the founder of the nonprofit Roots & Shoots global youth-led community action program, and the author of numerous books, including *Reason for Hope.*

SUBSCRIBE TO EVERYTHING WE PUBLISH!

Do you love what Microcosm publishes?

Do you want us to publish more great stuff?

Would you like to receive each new title as it's published?

Subscribe as a BFF to our new titles and we'll mail them all to you as they are released!

$10-30/mo, pay what you can afford. Include your t-shirt size and month/date of birthday for a possible surprise! Subscription begins the month after it is purchased.

microcosmpublishing.com/bff

     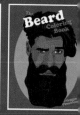